COLONIAL

JOBS

Verna Fisher

COLONIAL
QUEST

Nomad Press
A division of Nomad Communications
10 9 8 7 6 5 4 3 2 1

This book was manufactured by
Regal Printing Limited in China
June 2010, Job #1005018
ISBN: 978-1-936313-19-8

Illustrations by Andrew Christensen

Questions regarding the ordering of this book should be addressed to
Independent Publishers Group
814 N. Franklin St.
Chicago, IL 60610
www.ipgbook.com

Nomad Press
2456 Christian St.
White River Junction, VT 05001
www.nomadpress.net

Contents

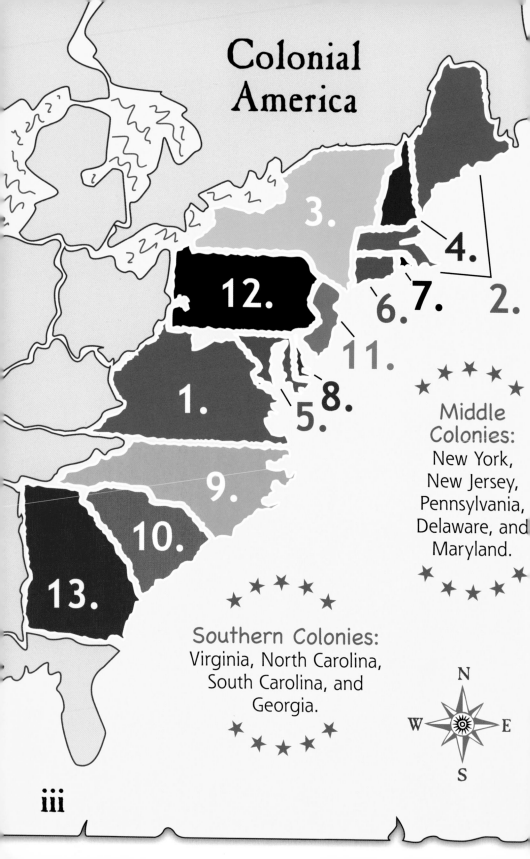

Colonial America

Middle Colonies: New York, New Jersey, Pennsylvania, Delaware, and Maryland.

Southern Colonies: Virginia, North Carolina, South Carolina, and Georgia.

N
W   E
S

New England:
Massachusetts,
New Hampshire, Connecticut,
and Rhode Island.

In the 1600s, people began leaving Europe to settle in America. Some were explorers searching for gold, while others came looking for freedom.

Jamestown in Virginia and Plymouth in Massachusetts were two of the earliest settlements where these people came to start a new life.

1607

1. Virginia

2. Massachusetts

3. New York

4. **New Hampshire**

5. Maryland

6. Connecticut

7. **Rhode Island**

8. **Delaware**

9. North Carolina

10. South Carolina

11. New Jersey

12. Pennsylvania

13. Georgia

Colonial Jobs Were Jobs Done By Hand

When the colonists came to the New World, they settled 13 colonies. These colonies were known as Colonial America.

The colonists made everything for themselves, from flour and iron horseshoes, to wooden buckets and furniture. Colonial jobs were very different from today's jobs! Colonists worked as cobblers, blacksmiths, coopers, cabinetmakers, millers, and in many other jobs.

Words to Know

colonist: a person who came to settle America.

New World: what is now America. It was called the New World by people from Europe because it was new to them.

colonies: early settlements in America.

Colonial America: the name given to this country when talking about the years 1607–1776.

Did You Know?

More than half the colonists came to the colonies as indentured servants. These servants had to work for seven years for the person who paid their way to the New World. After that, they could live and work where they pleased.

In colonial times many people learned a trade. It took long years of training to make goods by hand. Apprentices or indentured servants learned the trade while they helped craftsmen do their jobs.

Words to Know

trade: a job done by a person using his or her hands, learned through training and experience.

goods: things to use or sell.

apprentice: a person training in a trade.

craftsmen: skilled people in a trade who make a certain type of good.

4

During colonial times, many people were captured in Africa and forced to come to America to work as slaves. These people could not earn their freedom. The children of slaves were automatically slaves, too, and could be sold by their owners.

Some slaves worked for craftsmen, but many more worked on large farms in the south called plantations. Plantation owners mainly grew cotton and tobacco. These crops required a lot of work to grow and harvest.

slave: a person owned by another person and forced to work without pay, against their will.

Words to Know

Slavery in America ended after the Civil War in 1865.

Then and Now

In colonial times everything was made by hand because there was no electricity.

Today we have electricity, and most of the things we use every day are made in factories using machines.

6

Jobs at Home

The colonists grew a lot of their own food. They also made many goods at home. For example, they might weave their own fabric from cotton or wool thread and sew it into clothes. Cotton grows on the cotton plant. Wool comes from the coat of sheep.

Women and girls spun cotton and wool fibers into thread on a spinning wheel. This thread was washed and dyed, and then woven into fabric on a loom.

Women made large numbers of candles for light. Candle making was hard work. Sometimes the women used scented oils or berries to make their candles smell nice when they were burned.

The spinning wheel pulled on the fibers and twisted them into thread.

To make the candles, the women dipped wicks, or pieces of string, into hot wax over and over again, until the candles were a good size.

The Miller

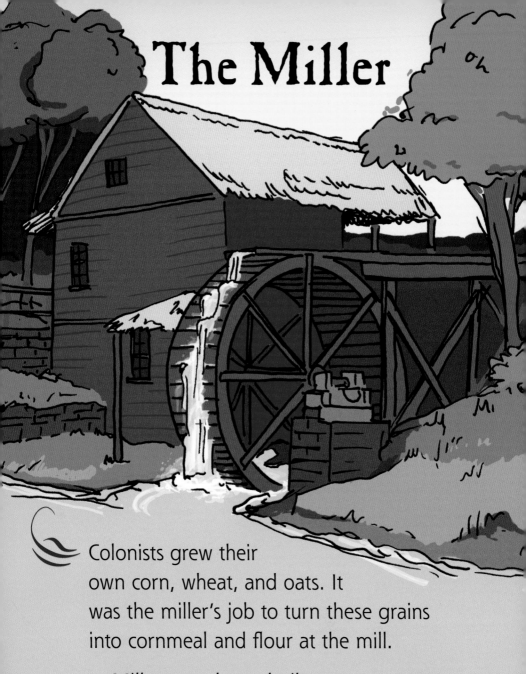

Colonists grew their own corn, wheat, and oats. It was the miller's job to turn these grains into cornmeal and flour at the mill.

Mills were always built next to streams. As the water from the stream ran over the mill's large wooden wheel, the water turned the wheel.

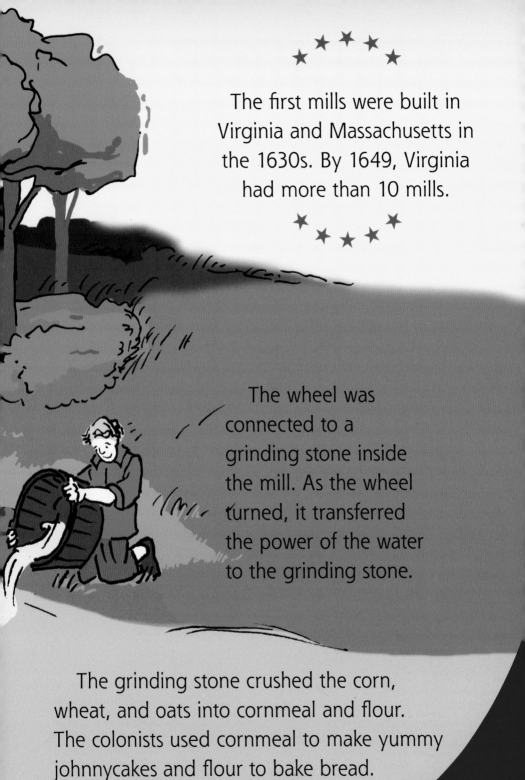

The first mills were built in Virginia and Massachusetts in the 1630s. By 1649, Virginia had more than 10 mills.

The wheel was connected to a grinding stone inside the mill. As the wheel turned, it transferred the power of the water to the grinding stone.

The grinding stone crushed the corn, wheat, and oats into cornmeal and flour. The colonists used cornmeal to make yummy johnnycakes and flour to bake bread.

The Blacksmith

The blacksmith made things out of iron. Nearly everyone in Colonial America had horses, and horses needed horseshoes to protect the bottom of their hoofs. Blacksmiths also made nails, tools, and cooking pots.

First the blacksmith heated the **iron** until it was soft enough to shape. Then he shaped it by hammering it against an **anvil**.

iron: a common metal.

anvil: a solid block.

Words to Know

The Cooper

Coopers made all kinds of wooden containers. Wooden barrels in lots of different sizes were used to store meat, corn, sugar, and flour.

★Then and Now

In colonial times, people used containers such as barrels and tubs made out of wood.

Today many of our containers are made out of plastic.

Buckets could be used to carry water and tubs were perfect for washing laundry and bathing.

First a cooper carved strips of wood. Then the wood was bent into shape and held tightly together by iron hoops. The iron hoops were made by the blacksmith.

Coopers made their containers so well that they even held liquids without leaking.

14

The Carpenter and the Cabinet Maker

When the colonists first arrived
in the New World they built
their own homes and furniture
as best they could. Most had
little skill in these jobs. As the
colonies grew, carpenters and
cabinet makers took over.

Most buildings were made of wood, and carpenters built homes and shops, as well as sheds and stables for horses. They were also kept busy repairing old buildings and building additions to them.

Cabinetmakers made furniture. They built chairs, tables, and desks, as well as chests of drawers for clothing. Early colonial furniture was often simple and plain.

As many colonists grew wealthy, they wanted fancier furniture. The designs resembled styles from England.

The Cobbler and the Tanner

Cobblers made and repaired shoes. Because new shoes were expensive, cobblers stayed busy repairing old, worn-out shoes. Most shoes were made from **leather**.

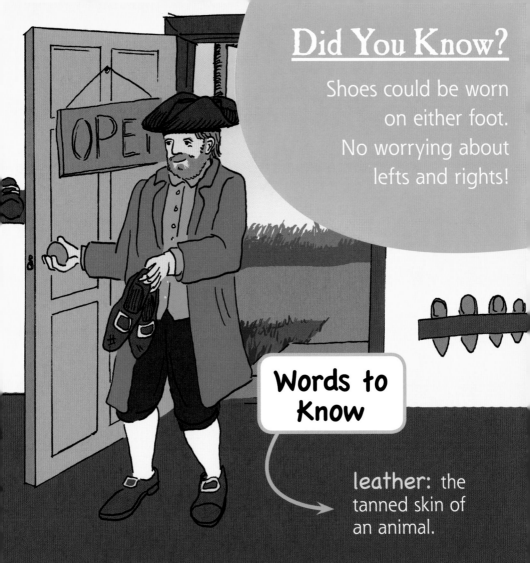

OPE[N]

Words to Know

leather: the tanned skin of an animal.

Tanners turned animal skins into leather. Tanning was a long process that involved scraping, soaking, and washing the skins many times. The colonists used leather for shoes, belts, bags, and saddles.

The Milliner

Milliners were women who owned shops that sold fabric. They also sold fancy items from Europe such as gloves, hats, shoes, and jewelry. Milliners mended clothing and made hats, aprons, cloaks and muffs.

cloak: a blanket-like coat worn over the shoulders like a cape.

muff: a fur sleeve, with two open ends.

custom made: made just for you.

Tailors made clothes for men and women. Coats, shirts, and breeches were custom made, even for boys.

On cold days, colonial women put their hands into the muff for warmth. Many milliners also made gowns. A person who made gowns was called a mantua maker.

The Wigmaker

Wigmakers ran shops that were like today's barber shops or hair salons. Men could get a shave and women could get their hair done.

Wealthy men and women began wearing wigs even if they had hair, trying to be in style.

Wigmakers also made wigs out of horse, goat, yak, or human hair. Wigs became popular after King Louis XIII of France started wearing one because he was losing his hair.

Wigs were very expensive. The wigmaker sewed curled hair into a cap custom made to fit the customer's head. The most formal wigs had white hair, with a ribbon tied around a ponytail or braid in the back. People put powder and perfume onto their wigs.

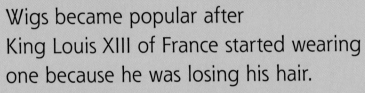

Trading With the Native Americans

The colonists traded food, furs, and other supplies with the Native Americans. The Native Americans were skilled at making many goods. Their canoes were made from hollowed-out trees or from birch tree bark sewn around wooden frames.

Native Americans made toboggans and snowshoes to travel on snow. Hunters brought food back to their villages on toboggans.

The Native Americans also made beautiful baskets and leather clothing. They used their basket-weaving skills to make mats, clothing, traps, and nets for fishing.

At first, the colonists did not use money. Instead, they traded one thing for another. Why did the colonists trade? Gold and silver coins were so rare in the colonies, trading made sense. Sometimes the colonists used wampum as a kind of money.

Glossary

anvil: a solid block.

apprentice: a person training in a trade.

blacksmith: a person who makes things out of iron.

cabinet maker: a person who makes furniture.

carpenter: a person who builds homes and other buildings out of wood.

cloak: a coat worn over the shoulders like a cape.

cobbler: a person who makes and repairs shoes.

Colonial America: the name given to this country when talking about the years 1607–1776.

colonies: early settlements in America.

colonist: a person who came to settle America.

cooper: a person who makes wooden containers.

craftsmen: skilled people in a trade who make a certain type of good.

custom made: made just for you.

dye: to make a color.

fibers: fine, short threads. Fibers twisted together make long strands of yarn and thread.

goods: things to use or sell.

iron: a common metal.

leather: the tanned skin of an animal.

loom: a large machine used to weave thread into fabric.

milliner: a person who sells fabric, hats, and other fashion accessories.

miller: a person who grinds grain into flour.

muff: a fur sleeve, with two open ends.

New World: what is now America. It was called the New World by people from Europe because it was new to them.

slave: a person owned by another person and forced to work without pay, against their will.

tanner: a person who makes leather.

trade: a job done by a person using his or her hands, learned through training and experience.

Further Investigations

Books

Bordessa, Kris. *Great Colonial America Projects You Can Build Yourself.* White River Junction, VT: Nomad Press, 2006.

Fisher, Verna. *Explore Colonial America! 25 Great Projects, Activities, Experiments.* White River Junction, VT: Nomad Press, 2009.

Museums and Websites

Colonial Williamsburg
www.history.org
Williamsburg, Virginia

National Museum of the American Indian
www.nmai.si.edu
Washington, D.C. and New York, New York

Plimoth Plantation
www.plimoth.org
Plymouth, Massachusetts

America's Library
www.americaslibrary.gov

Jamestown Settlement
www.historyisfun.org

Native American History
www.bigorrin.org

Native Languages of the Americas
www.native-languages.org

Social Studies for Kids
www.socialstudiesforkids.com

The Mayflower
www.mayflowerhistory.com

Virtual Jamestown
www.virtualjamestown.org

Index